ELECTIONS

PRESIDENTS
CAMPAIGNS
GOVERNMENT

Amanda Bennett

This book belongs to

_____

Elections:
Presidents, Campaigns, Government

ISBN 1-888306-18-1

Copyright © 1996 by Amanda Bennett

Published by:
Homeschool Press
229 S. Bridge St.
P.O. Box 254
Elkton, MD 21922-0254

Send requests for information to the above address.

Cover design by Mark Dinsmore.

Printed in the United States of America.

For my mom,

the encourager and motivator that the Lord knew I needed.

Thanks for sharing your love for people, politics,

and your adventures on the Hill.

How To Use This Guide

Welcome to the world of unit studies! They present a wonderful method of learning for all ages and it is a great pleasure to share this unit study with you. This guide has been developed and written to provide a basic framework for the study, along with plenty of ideas and resources to help round out the learning adventure. All the research is done. These are READY to go!

TO BEGIN: The <u>Outline</u> is the study "skeleton", providing an overall view of the subject and important subtopics. It can be your starting point—read through it and familiarize yourself with the content. It is great for charting your course over the next few weeks (or developing lesson plans). Please understand that you do not necessarily have to proceed through the outline in order. I personally focus on the areas that our children are interested in first—giving them "ownership" of the study. By beginning with their interest areas, it gives us the opportunity to further develop these interests while stretching into other areas of the outline as they increase their topic knowledge.

By working on a unit study for five or six weeks at a time, you can catch the children's attention and hold it for valuable learning. I try to wrap up each unit study in five or six weeks, whether or not we have "completed" the unit outline. The areas of the outline that we did not yet cover may be covered the next time we delve into the unit study topic (in a few months or perhaps next year). These guides are <u>non-consumable</u>—you can use them over and over again, covering new areas of interest as you review the previous things learned in the process.

The <u>Reading and Reference Lists</u> are lists of resources that feed right into various areas of the <u>Outline</u>. The books are listed with grade level recommendations and all the information that you need to locate them in the library or from your favorite book retailer. You can also order them through the national Inter-Library Loan System (I.L.L.)—check with the reference librarian at your local library.

There are several other components that also support the unit study.

The <u>Spelling and Vocabulary Lists</u> identify words that apply directly to the unit study, and are broken down into both Upper and Lower Levels for use with several ages.

The <u>Suggested Software, Games and Videos Lists</u> includes games, software and videos that make the learning fun, while reinforcing some of the basic concepts studied.

The <u>Activities and Field Trip Lists</u> include specific activity materials and field trip ideas that can be used with this unit to give some hands-on learning experience.

The <u>Internet Resources List</u> identifies sites that you might find helpful with this unit. The Internet is a wonderful resource to use with unit studies providing the sights and sounds of things that you might never otherwise experience! You can see works of art in the Louvre. See the sunrise on Mt. Rushmore, hear the sounds of the seashore and find many other things that will help provide an "immersion" in the unit study topic, as never before, without ever leaving home. As with any resource, use it with care and be there with the students as they go exploring new learning opportunities.

The author and the publisher care about you and your family. While not all of the materials recommended in this guide are written from a Christian perspective, they all have great educational value. Please use caution when using any materials. It's important to take the time to review books, games, and Internet sites before your children use them to make sure they meet your family's expectations.

As you can see, all of these sections have been included to help you build your unit study into a fun and fruitful learning adventure. Unit studies provide an excellent learning tool and give the students lifelong memories about the topic and the study.

Lots of phone numbers and addresses have been included to assist you in locating specific books and resources. To the best of our knowledge, all of these numbers were correct at the time of printing.

The left-hand pages of this book have been left "almost" blank for your notes, resources, ideas, children's artwork, or diagrams from this study or for ideas that you might like to pursue the next time you venture into this unit.

"Have fun &
Enjoy the Adventure!"

Table of Contents

Introduction

Speak up! Didn't you hear that often in your formative years—from adults who were encouraging you to say what was on your mind and communicate your ideas? I know first-hand as a parent, we encourage speaking up in our own children. As American citizens, we also need to speak up in our government and articulate our opinions clearly through participating in elections, as well as other outlets. As these children of ours grow up and become adults in our communities, they need to be aware and informed of the election process, the workings of American government and ways that they can impact the process.

With this unit study, your family can learn so much about elections, including:

- History of elections
- Basic structure of representative government
- Voting and election process
- Campaign participation and opportunities
- Basics of statistics and how they are used in campaigns and elections
- Presidents, their families and their opponents

God's mighty hand can be seen throughout the history of this country and its elections. It is up to us to acknowledge this and share the vision with our children. As the members of this generation mature, they need to be fully aware of their own capabilities and responsibilities within the framework of our American government. This unit study can open the doors to further learning and understanding in these areas. It will get the whole family involved in elections and politics. We parents need to stay aware of issues that affect us in our efforts. Students need to understand that they, too, will need to stay involved in the process to protect and maintain our guaranteed freedoms.

Make learning about this great country a wonderful and interesting adventure. Instead of learning about elections and government from a dry textbook, enjoy the process and use real books. Discover exciting elections, unpredictable outcomes and read biographies on various Presidents and their own family lives.

This unit study offers a glimpse of all these things and more. Starting with the younger students, you can have a great deal of fun delving into some history of the Constitution and learn more about Presidents like George Washington and Abraham Lincoln. The older students can study the U. S. Constitution and its origins. From this, they will get an excellent understanding of the basic structure of our government. They can go into detail in their study of the election process and past and present candidates. Pursue this study on a regular basis throughout your children's education. You can cover different sections each time that you repeat Elections. This will provide a solid knowledge base in history and government, and strengthen your students' understanding of their rights and responsibilities.

Use this Elections study to inform and empower the next generation! Enjoy the adventure; as well as the election!

Study Outline

I. Introduction

    A.   The meaning and origin of the word "election"

    B.   Why it is important to study and understand elections

        1.   To understand how the government framework is designed to work

        2.   To learn about the history of our country and its elected officials

        3.   To understand the campaign process, candidates' viewpoints and the importance of issues

        4.   To become a part of the American government, by voicing opinions and convictions to our representatives at all levels

II. Government basics

    A.   The Constitution

        1.   The drafting of the Constitution

            a.   The convention and attending delegates

            b.   Plans proposed for the new agreement

        2.   The Great Compromise

        3.   Ratification

        4.   The Bill of Rights

        5.   Constitutional Amendments

    B.   Three main branches of American government

        1.   Executive Branch

            a.   President

            b.   Vice President

            c.   Cabinet

        2.   Legislative Branch

            a.   House of Representatives

            b.   Senate

        3.   Judicial Branch

            a.   Supreme Court

            b.   Federal Court System

III. Government by representation

A. The right to vote
  1. Voting was originally restricted to white men that owned property or had considerable wealth
  2. The Fifteenth Amendment to the Constitution
     a. This amendment made it illegal to block citizens from voting because of race
     b. Poll tax and literacy tests were used to get around this amendment
  3. The Nineteenth Amendment to the Constitution gave women the right to vote
  4. The Twenty-fourth Amendment to the Constitution forbid the use of poll tax to deny a citizen the right to vote
  5. The Twenty-sixth Amendment lowered the minimum voting age to eighteen years of age.
B. National elections
  1. Presidential elections
     a. Popular vote election
     b. Electoral College vote
  2. Congressional elections
  3. Election Day—the first Tuesday after the first Monday in November
C. State elections
  1. Governor
  2. State congressional representatives
  3. State offices
     a. Insurance Commissioner
     b. Treasury
D. Local elections
  1. Commissioners
  2. Mayor
  3. Sheriff
  4. Local issues
     a. Zoning/Planning
     b. Taxes
     c. Referendums
E. Special elections

IV. The structure of an election

A. Political parties
   1. Platform
   2. Candidates
   3. Voter appeal
   4. Caucuses and primaries
B. Candidates
   1. Must meet qualifications for the desired position
      a. President
      b. Senate seat
      c. House of Representatives seat
   2. Develop their stances on various key election issues
      a. Laws
      b. Taxes
      c. Rights
      d. Economy
      e. Goals
      f. Special interests
C. Campaigns
   1. Notable historic campaigns
      a. Election of Thomas Jefferson in 1800—two-party system is firmly established
      b. Election of Andrew Jackson in 1828—marking the beginning of the importance of the popular vote
      c. Election of Abraham Lincoln in 1860—split the party system and marked the beginning of the secession of Southern states
   2. Structure of a campaign
      a. Local or state election
      b. National election
   3. The campaign process for the candidate
      a. Organize a campaign staff
         (1) Campaign manager
         (2) Advance team
         (3) Media contact
         (4) Fund-raiser
         (5) Speech writer

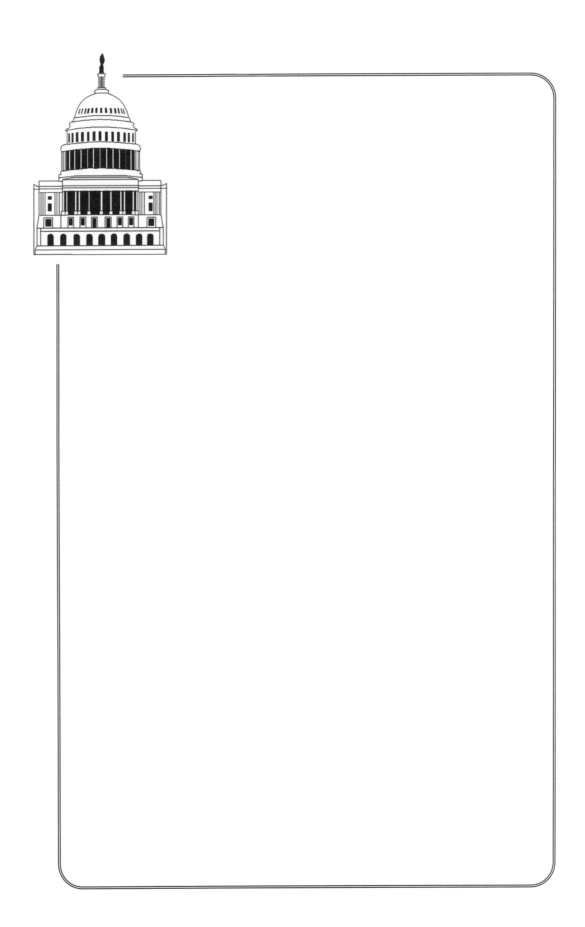

           b.   Begin fund-raising efforts
           c.   Develop an agenda and issues position
           d.   Consult with a pollster to get feedback on issues relevant to your constituents
           e.   Meet with the public
                (1)   Develop recognition
                (2)   Get feedback on issues
                (3)   Test new ideas
                (4)   Refine political image
      4.   Raising financing for the campaign
           a.   Federal Elections Campaign Act (1971)
           b.   Political action committees (PACs)
           c.   Candidate's personal efforts and funds
           d.   Political party efforts
           e.   Reporting to the Federal Elections Commission

V.   Voting

A.   Definition of "vote" and "suffrage"
B.   Each citizen's opportunity to have an impact on our government
     1.   Right to vote is guaranteed
     2.   History of the vote
          a.   Early American voting procedures
          b.   Australian ballot acceptance
C.   Voter registration
     1.   Eligible voters
          a.   Residency requirements
          b.   18 years of age or older
     2.   Ineligible voters
          a.   Citizens of other countries
          b.   People convicted of felonies
          c.   Mentally incompetent people
D.   Casting the vote
     1.   The voting machines
     2.   The ballot
     3.   Absentee ballot
E.   The vote count
F.   Reporting the election results
     1.   Media coverage
     2.   Victory and defeat speeches

VI. American Political Parties

A. History of political parties in America
    1. Federalist party
    2. Anti-Federalist party
    3. Democratic Republican party
    4. National Republican party
    5. Democratic party
    6. Whig party

B. Modern-day political parties
    1. Republican party
    2. Democratic party
    3. Third parties

VII. Presidents of the United States

A. George Washington
    1. In office from 1789 - 1797
    2. Elected unanimously by the Electoral College

B. John Adams
    1. In office from 1797 - 1801
    2. Federalist Party

C. Thomas Jefferson
    1. In office from 1801 - 1809
    2. Democratic-Republican Party

D. James Madison
    1. In office from 1809 - 1817
    2. Democratic-Republican Party

E. James Monroe
    1. In office from 1817 - 1825
    2. Democratic-Republican Party

F. John Quincy Adams
    1. In office from 1825 - 1829
    2. Democratic-Republican Party

G. Andrew Jackson
    1. In office from 1829 - 1837
    2. Democratic Party

H. Martin Van Buren
    1. In office from 1837 - 1841
    2. Democratic Party

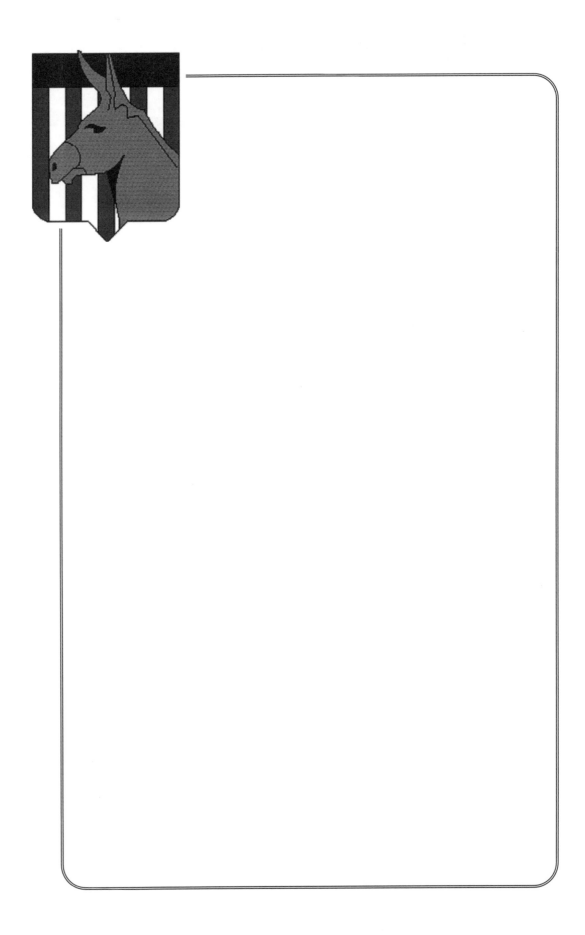

I. William Henry Harrison
   1. In office 1841
   2. Whig Party
J. John Tyler
   1. In office from 1841 - 1845
   2. Whig Party
K. James K. Polk
   1. In office from 1845 - 1849
   2. Democratic Party
L. Zachary Taylor
   1. In office from 1849 - 1850
   2. Whig Party
M. Millard Fillmore
   1. In office from 1850 - 1853
   2. Whig Party
N. Franklin Pierce
   1. In office from 1853 - 1857
   2. Democratic Party
O. James Buchanan
   1. In office from 1857 - 1861
   2. Democratic Party
P. Abraham Lincoln
   1. In office from 1861 - 1865
   2. Republican Party
Q. Andrew Johnson
   1. In office from 1865 - 1869
   2. Democratic Party
R. Ulysses S. Grant
   1. In office from 1869 - 1877
   2. Republican Party
S. Rutherford B. Hayes
   1. In office from 1877 - 1881
   2. Republican Party
T. James A. Garfield
   1. In office in 1881
   2. Republican Party
U. Chester A. Arthur
   1. In office from 1881 - 1885
   2. Republican Party

V.   Grover Cleveland
  1.   In office from 1885 - 1889, and again from 1893 - 1897
  2.   Democratic Party
W.   Benjamin Harrison
  1.   In office from 1889 - 1893
  2.   Republican Party
X.   William McKinley
  1.   In office from 1897 - 1901
  2.   Republican Party
Y.   Theodore Roosevelt
  1.   In office from 1901 - 1909
  2.   Republican Party
Z.   William H. Taft
  1.   In office from 1909 - 1913
  2.   Republican Party
AA.   Woodrow Wilson
  1.   In office from 1913 - 1921
  2.   Democratic Party
BB.   Warren G. Harding
  1.   In office from 1921 - 1923
  2.   Republican Party
CC.   Calvin Coolidge
  1.   In office from 1923 - 1929
  2.   Republican Party
DD.   Herbert Hoover
  1.   In office from 1929 - 1933
  2.   Republican Party
EE.   Franklin D. Roosevelt
  1.   In office from 1933 - 1945
  2.   Democratic Party
FF.   Harry S. Truman
  1.   In office from 1945 - 1953
  2.   Democratic Party
GG.   Dwight D. Eisenhower
  1.   In office from 1953 - 1961
  2.   Republican Party
HH.   John F. Kennedy
  1.   In office from 1961 - 1963
  2.   Democratic Party

II.   Lyndon B. Johnson
   1.   In office from 1963 - 1969
   2.   Democratic Party
JJ.   Richard M. Nixon
   1.   In office from 1969 - 1974
   2.   Republican Party
KK.   Gerald R. Ford
   1.   In office from 1974 - 1977
   2.   Republican Party
LL.   Jimmy Carter
   1.   In office from 1977 - 1981
   2.   Democratic party
MM.   Ronald Reagan
   1.   In office from 1981 - 1989
   2.   Republican Party
NN.   George Bush
   1.   In office from 1989 - 1993
   2.   Republican Party
OO.   William Clinton
   1.   In office from 1993 - present
   2.   Democratic Party

VIII. The arts and elections

A.   Campaign designs—buttons, banners, etc.
B.   Musical slogans, songs, etc.
C.   Candidate images—photos, paintings, media portrayal
D.   Collectible campaign items

Spelling/Vocabulary List

Lower Level

act

age

agree

alien

alike

ballot

band

bill

booth

card

change

choose

citizen

city

close

count

country

county

differ

different

elect

equal

fact

free

freedom

honor

issue

keep

law

left

lose

mail

men

need

party

pick

politics

poll

promise

right

rule

rural

secret

smart

speak

speech

state

tax

think

town

truth

urban

victory

voice

vote

want

win

wise

women

wrong

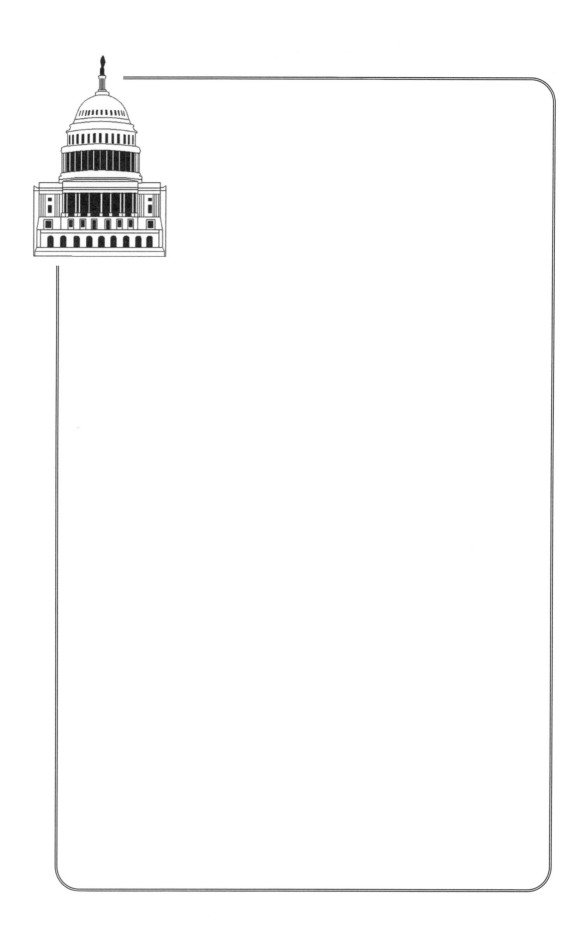

Spelling/Vocabulary List

Upper Level

absentee ballot
advertisement
agencies
alien
attorney general
ballot
bandwagon
Bill of Rights
bipartisan
blitz

Cabinet
campaign
candidate
caucus
chairman
choice
citizen
city
civics
civil rights

claim
committee
Congress
conservative
Constitution
convention
country
county clerk
county
debate

delegate
democracy
democratic
district attorney
district
donation
elect
election
eligible
endorsement

Executive Office
experience
financial statement
govern
government
governor
Senate
House of Representatives
independent
indicators

initiative
issues
judge
keynote speech
legislate
legislature
liberal
lieutenant governor
local
majority

mayor
media
minority
national
nominations
Oath of Office
opposed
partisan
petition
platform

political parties
political science
poll tax
polling place
polls
popular vote
precinct
President
primary
protest

public opinion survey
qualifications
qualify
referendum
represent
Representative
republic
republican
requirements
runoff

Senate
Senator
sheriff
slogan
smear tactic
split-ticket
state
statistics
straight-ticket
suffrage

superintendent
Supreme Court
tax assessor
town council
turnout
Vice President
volunteer
voter apathy
voter registration
voter turnout

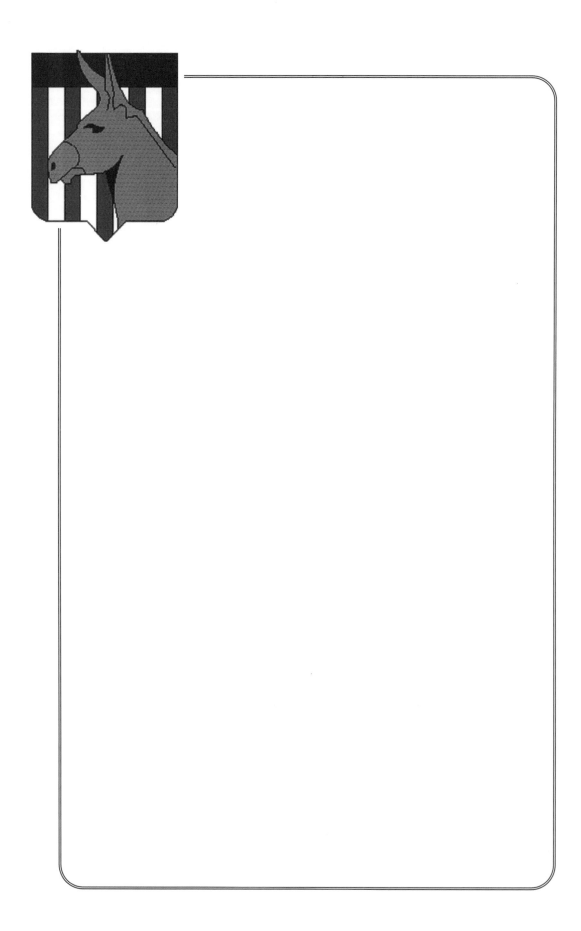

Writing Ideas

Here are some ideas to help incorporate writing in a unit study. Choose one or two and watch what happens!

1. Issues—what issues are important to your family in the upcoming elections? Have your students determine the issues that are important to them, and explain why. Consider having them interview family members about the issues that they are most concerned with during the upcoming election. The student can summarize their findings in a written report, possibly in a family newsletter format.

2. It is always interesting to have the student compose and write letters to various people and organizations that pertain to the unit study. Here are a few addresses to give you some ideas:

    The Republican National Party
    Republican National Committee
    310 First St. S.E.
    Washington, DC 20003
    (202) 863-8885

    The Democratic National Party
    Democratic National Committee
    430 South Capitol St. S.E.
    Washington, DC 20003
    (202) 863-8000

    Project Vote Smart
    129 NW 4th St. #204
    Corvallis, OR 97330
    (800) 622-SMART

    The White House
    1600 Pennsylvania Ave., N.W.
    Washington, D.C. 20500
    (202) 456-1414

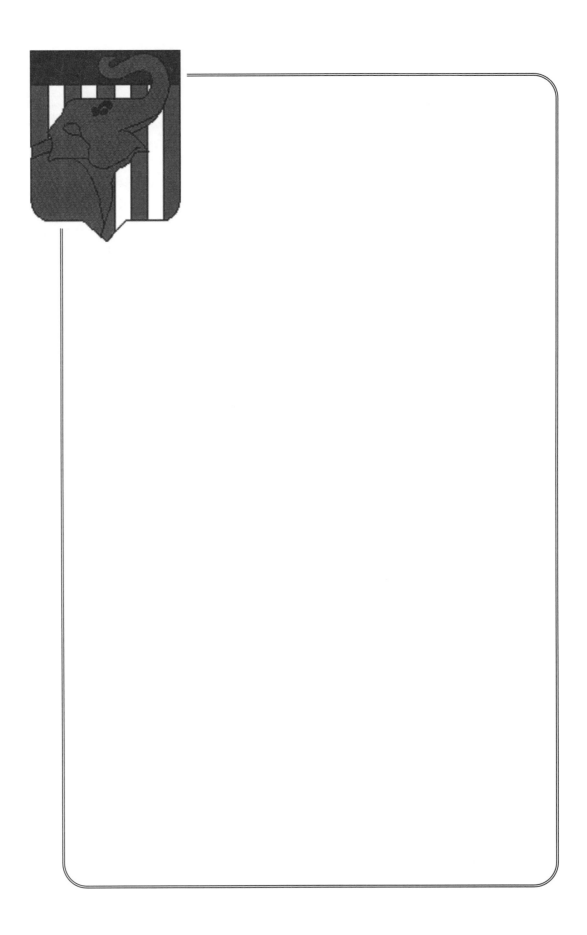

The Federal Election Commission
999 E Street N.W.
Washington, DC 20463
(800) 424-9530

The League of Women Voters Education Fund
1730 M Street N.W.
Washington, DC 20036
(202) 429-1965

3. As the campaign gets underway, have the students keep a journal of their favorite candidate's activities for the day. They can use newspaper clippings, the local television news or any other sources for tracking the candidate. After the election, they can summarize the election result to conclude their project and have some interesting souvenirs of their elections unit study.

Activity Ideas

Activities provide a great way to reinforce the material that we learn in a unit study. They provide important hands-on learning while we have fun are challenged at the same time. As we work on a unit, we use activities like those listed in the Activity Resources, as well as some of our own ideas to provide some hands-on learning. Here are a few activity ideas to get you started. Don't be surprised if the children come up with some great ones of their own!

1. As you delve into the history of elections, have the students select one of the actual elections and candidates that they are interested in studying in-depth. Using the library, your home book collection, the Internet and other resources, help them investigate the event and the people. On the Internet, you can even find each Inaugural Address!

2. Find out how each candidate stands on important issues—write or call his/her office and get a statement of opinion or written policy/platform on key issues.

3. Contact the Superintendent of Elections to get any information available by mail for the upcoming elections, find out what issues will be on the ballot, when the primaries are, etc. For more information on your particular area, contact your local librarian.

4. Learn to play chess—it is a wonderful way to develop thinking skills (like strategy, prediction, etc.) as well as to learn this classic game that has been passed down through the ages. Take some time to investigate the history of chess. A good game of chess frequently reminds me of a political match—they contain the same thought processes and planning strategies. For more information about chess, write: **United States Chess Federation**, 186 Route 9W, New Windsor, NY 12553. (800) 388-KING.

Job Opportunities

Here is a list of jobs that involve some of the aspects of elections, campaigns and political science. There are others that I'm sure you will identify.

Administrative aide	Photographer
Attorney	Political scientist
Banking specialist	Political party worker
Campaign manager	Politician
Computer scientist	President
Council member	Psychologist
Criminal investigator	Public relations specialist
Editor	Radio broadcaster
Foreign service official	Reporter
Governor	Representative
Historian	Sales
Information specialist	Senator
Judge	Sheriff
Legislative aide	Social worker
Lieutenant Governor	Speech writer
Lobbyist	Staff manager
Magazine writer/reporter	Statistician
Mayor	Superintendent of voting
Media specialist	Supreme Court Justice
Museum curator	Television writer
Newspaper writer/reporter	Television reporter
Pastor	

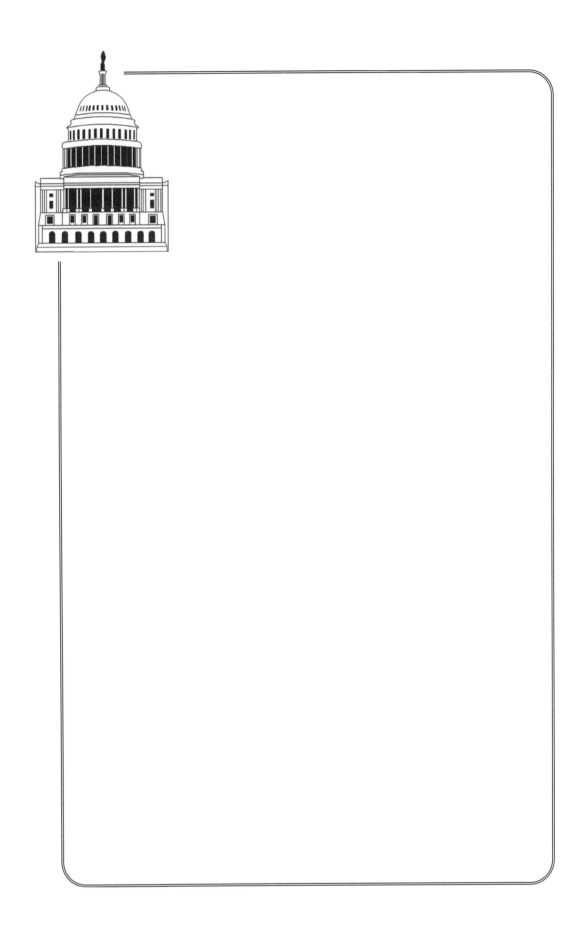

For more information about these jobs or others that may be interesting, go to the reference librarian in the public library and ask for publications on careers. Some that we recommend are:

The Encyclopedia of Careers and Vocational Guidance, published by J. G. Ferguson Publishing Company, Chicago.

Occupational Outlook Handbook, published by the US Department of Labor, Bureau of Labor Statistics. It presents detailed information on 250 occupations that employ the vast majority of workers. It describes the nature of work, training and educational requirements, working conditions and earnings potential.

Room Decorations

We usually try to decorate our den around the theme of the current unit study. For the election theme, there are plenty of decorations that can be made or purchased inexpensively. Here are a few to get you started:

1. Campaign posters are usually available from many of the candidates and political parties for the asking. They usually make available posters, flyers and yard signs.

2. Place a large U. S. map on the wall. Mark state primaries and caucuses with small notes and the dates of the events. Have the students track and list the results, as the events take place.

3. Make a wall chart of each of the state and territory primaries and caucuses. List each candidate that you and your family are interested in observing. Update the chart with the outcomes of each event.

4. Make a wall chart of issues that your students are interested in for the upcoming elections. List each candidates' statements concerning their stand on those issues as the campaign progresses.

5. Have the students design their own campaign banners and slogans for various candidates that they are interested in, whether local, state or national.

6. ***Our American History Poster Set*** is an inexpensive set of 16 posters (including George Washington, Bill of Rights, Branches of the governments, etc.) and is available from Farm Country General Store, Rt. 1, Box 63, Metamora, IL 61548. (800) 551-FARM.

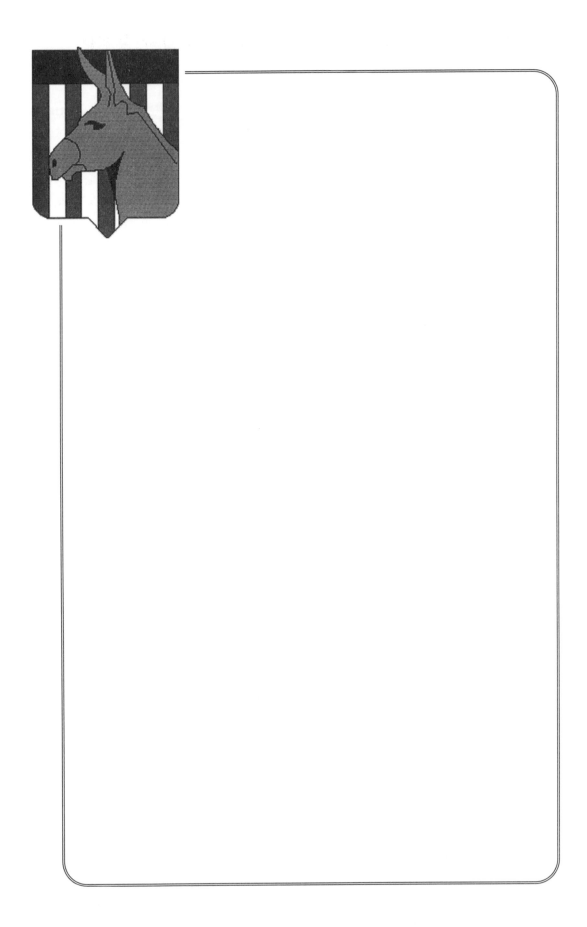

Games, Videos and Software

Games are a great way to reinforce the material that we learn. We have fun while reviewing important information and concepts around the kitchen table or on the computer. The software listed here is just a small sample of what is available. During the writing of this book, there have been several new games and software packages in development for release in the near future. All sound very exciting! Check around at your local toy and software stores to find out the latest introductions.

Hail to the Chief—is a board game that depicts the campaign trail, all the way through a Presidential election. It is available from: Aristoplay, P.O. Box 7529, Ann Arbor, Michigan 48107. (800) 634-7738.

Presidents card game—is also available from Aristoplay.

The Propaganda Game from WFF'N Proof. Available from Great Christian Books (800) 775-5422.

Presidential Rummy and ***Presidential Lotto*** from Safari Ltd. Available from Lifetime Books & Gifts, 3900 Chalet Suzanne Drive, Lake Wales, FL 33853. (800) 377-0390.

The Kids' Book of Chess, by Harvey Kidder. This book comes in a chess "kit" for children called **The Kids' Chess Set** that also includes a chess gameboard and pieces. Published by Workman Publishing Company. Available from Farm Country General Store, Rt. 1, Box 63, Metamora, IL 61548. (800) 551-FARM.

Videos:

While you learn about elections, look for the many great television broadcasts and videos available that relate to voting, government and the presidents. Many of these can be obtained through your local library or video store.

During a campaign season, there will be many opportunities to observe candidates on all levels, (local, state and national) through debates and news-hour broadcasts. The debates can be interesting, along with the commentaries that occur following the debates.

In addition, there are many great documentaries available on Public Broadcasting Stations (PBS) and through the library—like the series "**Abraham Lincoln.**" This series is broadcast periodically through PBS, and is comprised of four parts: "**The Making of a President,**" "**The Pivotal Year,**" "**I Want to Finish This Job**" and "**Now He Belongs to the Ages.**"

Questar Videos has also produced several videos that will add interest to your unit study. One of their video series is titled "**Presidents.**" Some libraries carry this series, or you can order it from Great Christian Books, (800) 775-5422.

There are also some older classic movies available that are fun to watch, while you work on the unit. Some to consider include "**Abe Lincoln in Illinois,** "**Young Mr. Lincoln**" and "**Mr. Smith Goes to Washington.**"

Software:

American History Explorer by Parsons Technology. (800) 223-6925. Grades 6 and up. It comes on CD-ROM and covers American history from 1000 A.D. up through the Reconstruction era. (For an in-depth review, see "Miscellaneous Reviews" in the October/November '95 issue of *Homeschool Computing*, (913) 363-7797)

Portraits of American Presidents by Great Bear Technology, 1100 Moraga Way, Moraga, CA 94556. Ages 10 and up. This CD-ROM combines NBC News footage, Questar video clips for a multimedia adventure through American History. Available from Great Christian Books (800) 775-5422.

Field Trip Ideas

There are so many field trips that can be enjoyed while learning about elections, that it is hard to list all of the ones that you might want to consider. Please use this list to get started planning some field trips, then let your imagination identify others that are in your area. Don't forget to take along your camera to capture some of the sights of the surroundings, as well as the children! Also, try to write the places that you visit and thank the hosts for their time. You can have one of the older children write thank-you notes.

1. Call the district or local offices of political parties in your area and ask about coming for a visit during their office hours. You might be able to meet some of their candidates in person, watch a telephone calling campaign in progress or watch a mass mailing project being prepared.

2. During election years, there are usually public sessions, debates and "meet the candidate" get-togethers. Find out when these are scheduled. Take your students along to watch the political process at the grass-roots level.

3. Have the older students select a candidate or two that they are interested in supporting. Find out if there are volunteer opportunities available within the campaigns of these candidates. Usually campaigns welcome help with telephones, letter stuffing, data entry, etc.

4. Plan a field trip to the local Superintendent of Elections, to see voting machines, tallying equipment, etc.

5. Find out if the League of Women Voters has any activities planned in your area to introduce the candidates, sponsor debates, etc—attending these will help introduce your students to the field of candidates, as well as the world of politics.

6. If you live within a reasonable drive of a state capitol or Washington, D.C., consider planning a day trip to visit the capitol buildings. You might observe the legislators in session! Many state capitols have a state history museum that would provide some interesting elections background.

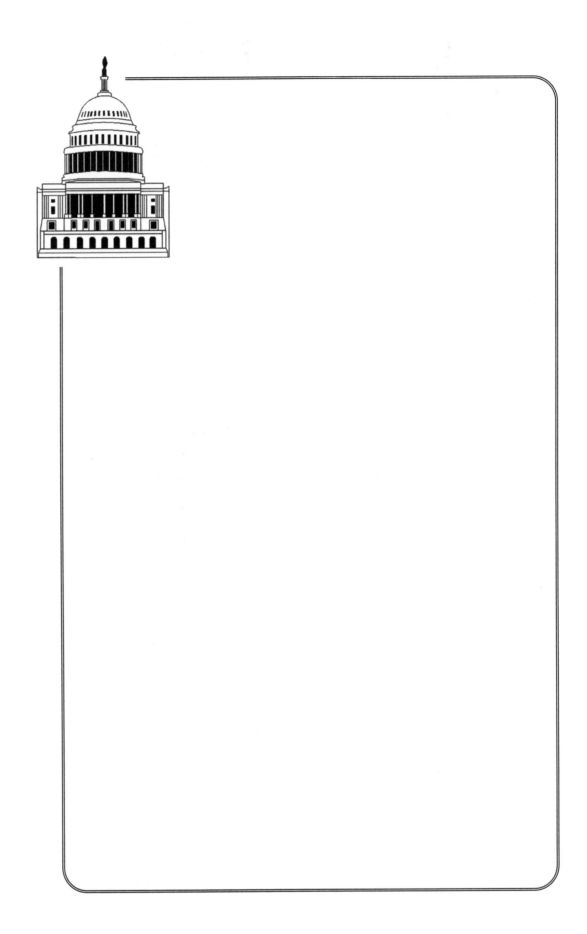

Subject Key Words

This list of SUBJECT search words has been included to help you with this unit study. To find material about elections and other related topics, go to the card catalog or computerized holdings catalog in your library and look up:

General Concepts:

amendment
Australian ballot
ballot
Board of Elections
Cabinet
campaign
candidate
Congress
conservative
Constitution
democracy
Democratic Political Party
Electoral College
Federal Election Commission
freedom
fund raising
government
governor
House of Representatives
Independent Political Party
leadership
left-wing
liberal
local government
national government
petition
platform
political action committee (PAC)
political party

president
primary
representation
republic
Republican Political Party
right-wing
Senate
state government
suffrage
vote count
voter registration

Famous People:

John Adams
John Quincy Adams
Chester A. Arthur
James Buchanan
George Bush
Grover Cleveland
William Clinton
Calvin Coolidge
Dwight D. Eisenhower
Millard Fillmore
Gerald R. Ford
James A. Garfield
Ulysses S. Grant
Warren G. Harding
Benjamin Harrison
William Henry Harrison
Rutherford B. Hayes

Herbert Hoover
Andrew Jackson
Thomas Jefferson
Andrew Johnson
Lyndon B. Johnson
John F. Kennedy
James Madison
William McKinley
James Monroe
Richard M. Nixon

James K. Polk
Franklin D. Roosevelt
Theodore Roosevelt
William H. Taft
Zachary Taylor
Harry S. Truman
John Tyler
Martin Van Buren
George Washington

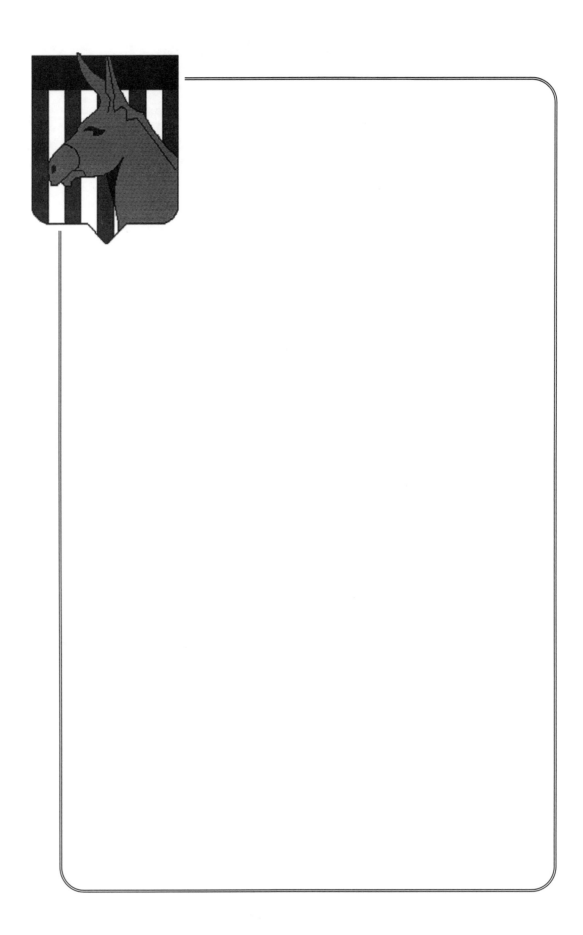

Trivia Questions

These questions have been included for fun. They reinforce some of the material that you might read during this study. Enjoy the search for answers, and then compare them with the answers that we found, located on page 61.

1. From what country did the current form of balloting in the United States originate?

2. What does the long-time nickname for the Republican Party, G.O.P., stand for?

3. Which election and what candidates used the following slogans?

   "The Square Deal"

   "Two Chickens in Every Pot"

   "The New Deal"

4. The delegates at what we now call the "Constitutional Convention" referred to the convention by two other names. What were the two names?

5. What small political party is credited with starting the tradition of holding national conventions to select political candidates?

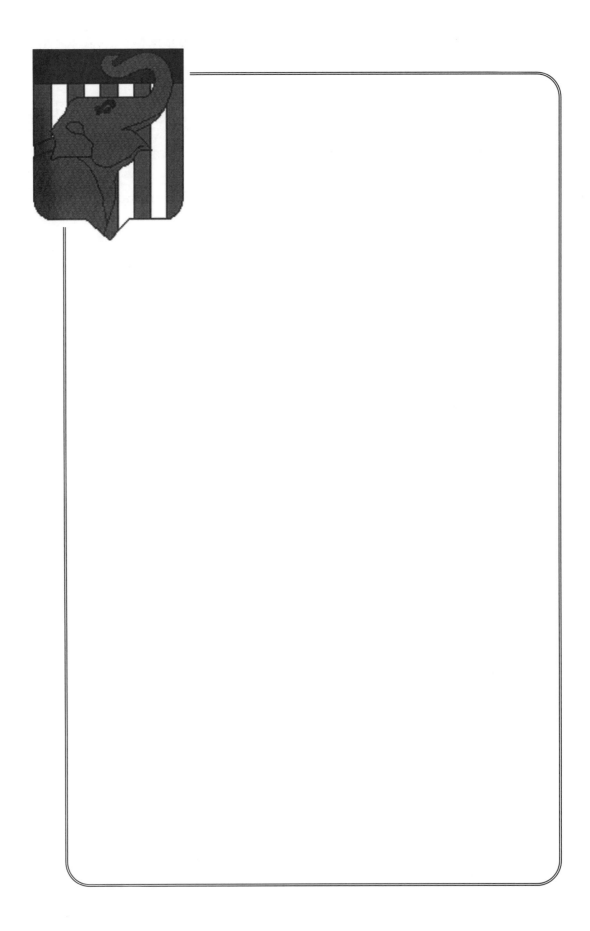

6. Which amendment to the Constitution made it legal for black males to vote?

7. Which amendment to the Constitution recognized the right of women to vote?

8. Which was the only amendment to the Constitution that was ever repealed?

9. Who was President of the United States when South Carolina seceded from the Union?

10. What happens if no candidate obtains a majority of votes in the Electoral College?

Trivia Answers

1. From what country did the current form of balloting in the United States originate?

   Australia

2. What does the long-time nickname for the Republican Party, G.O.P., stand for?

   Grand Old Party

3. Which election and what candidates used the following slogans?

   "The Square Deal"

   1904, Theodore Roosevelt

   "Two Chickens in Every Pot"

   1928, Herbert Hoover

   "The New Deal"

   1932, Franklin D. Roosevelt

4. The delegates at what we now call the "Constitutional Convention" referred to the convention by two other names. What were the two names?

   Grand Convention or Federal Convention

5. What small political party is credited with starting the tradition of holding national conventions to select political candidates?

   The Antimasons held national conventions in 1830 and 1831

6. Which amendment to the Constitution made it legal for black males to vote?

    The Fifteenth Amendment

7. Which amendment to the Constitution recognized the right of women to vote?

    The Nineteenth Amendment

8. Which was the only amendment to the Constitution that was ever repealed?

    The Eighteenth Amendment, also called the Prohibition Amendment

9. Who was President of the United States when South Carolina seceded from the Union?

    James Buchanan

10. What happens if no candidate obtains a majority of votes in the Electoral College?

    The Constitution provides that, in this case, the next President will be chosen by the House of Representatives.

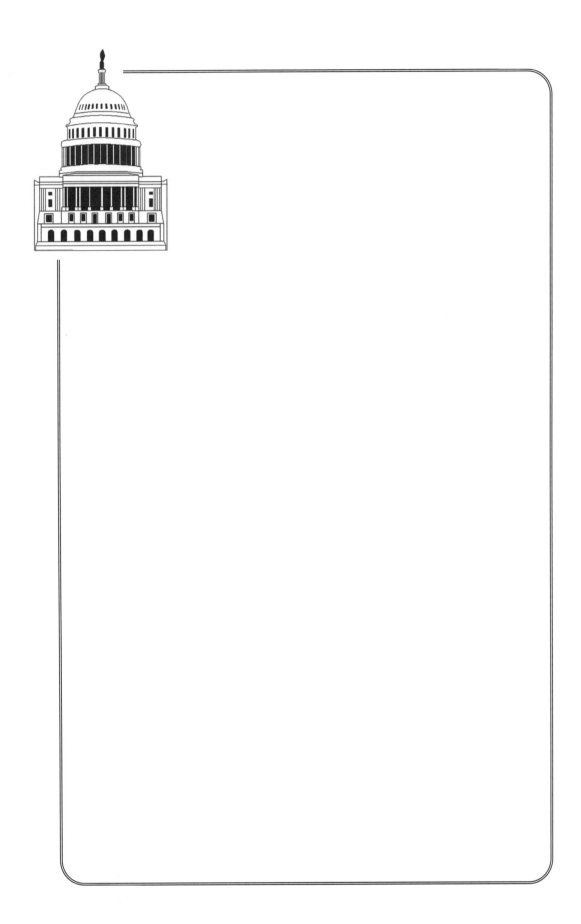

Reference Resources
History

The Story of Presidential Elections, by Jim Hargrove. (Cornerstones of Freedom Series). Grades 2 - 6. Published by Children's Press, PO Box 1331, Dambury, CT 06813. (800) 621-1115.

History of American Presidential Campaigns, by Arthur M. Schlesinger. Grades 7 - 12. Published by Chelsea House Publishers, 1974 Sproul Rd., Suite 400, PO Box 1914, Broomall, PA 19000. (800) 848-2665.

A Child's Story of America, published by Christian Liberty Press, 502 West Euclid Avenue, Arlington Heights, IL 60004. (708) 259-8736.

America, The First 350 Years, a tape series (16 tapes, as well as a notebook and study guide) written and narrated by Pastor Steve Wilkins. Grades 7 and up. Produced by Covenant Publications, 224 Auburn Ave., Monroe, LA 71201. (318) 323-3061.

Hail To The Candidate: Presidential Campaigns From Banners to Broadcasts, by Keith Melder. Grades 7 and up. Published by Smithsonian Institution Press, 470 L'Enfant Plaza, Suite 7100, Washington, DC 20560.

The World Almanac of Presidential Campaigns, by Eileen Shields-West. Grades 7 - 12. Published by World Almanac, 200 Park Avenue, New York, NY 10166.

Reference Resources
Elections

Electing a U.S. President, by Diana Reische. Grades 7 - 12. Published by Franklin Watts, 5450 Cumberland Ave., Chicago, IL 60656. (800) 672-6672.

Campaigns and Elections, (Ballots & Bandwagons Series). Grade 4 - 6. Published by Silver Burdett Press, Simon & Schuster, Inc., 200 Old Tappan Rd., Old Tappan, NJ 07675 (800) 257-5755.

It's A Free Country: A Young Person's Guide to Politics & Elections, by Cynthia K. Samuels. Grades 7 - 12. Published by Atheneum, Macmillan Publishing Company, 866 Third Ave., New York, NY 10022.

Presidential Campaign, by Thomas R. Raber. Grades 4 - 8. Published by Lerner Publications, 241 First Ave. N., Minneapolis, MN 55401. (800) 328-4929.

The Vote: Making Your Voice Heard, by Linda Scher. (Good Citizenship Series). Grades 4 - 8. Published by Raintree Steck-Vaughn, PO Box 26015, Austin, TX 78755. (800) 531-5015.

Our Elections, by Richard Steins. (I Know America Series). Grades 3 - 8. Published by Millbrook Press, 2 Old New Milford Rd., Brookfield, CT 06804. (800) 621-1115.

Voting and Elections, by Dennis B. Fradin. (A New True Book). Grades K - 3. Published by Children's Press, PO Box 1331, Danbury, CT 06813. (800) 621-1115.

The First Book of Elections, by Edmund Lindop. Grades 3 - 8. Published by Franklin Watts, 5450 Cumberland Ave., Chicago, IL 60656. (800) 672-6672.

Winners and Losers: How Elections Work in America, by Jules Archer. Grades 9 - 12. Published by Harcourt Brace Jovanovich, 6277 Sea Harbor Drive, Orlando, FL 32886. (800) 782-4479.

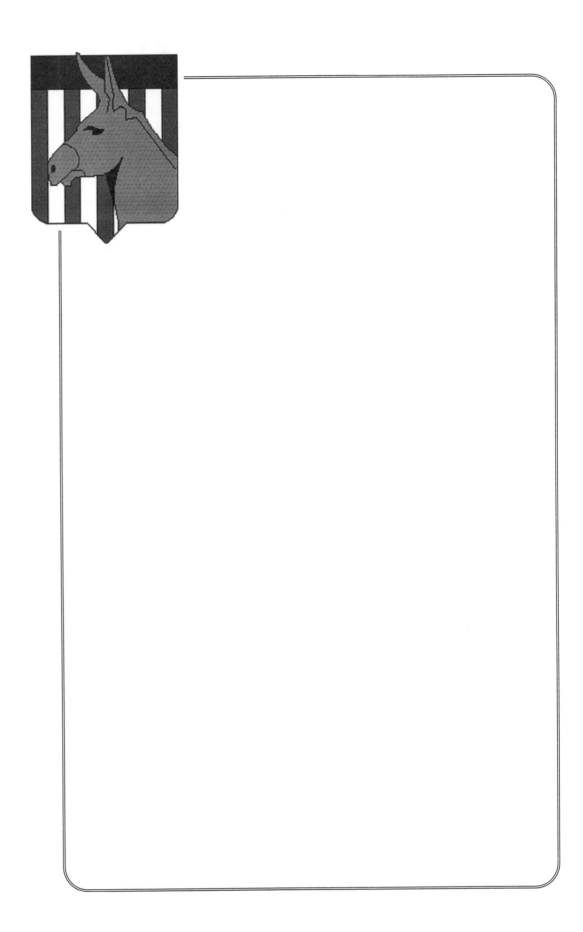

Politics in America: Opposing Viewpoints, by David Bender and Bruno Leone. Grades 10-12. Published by Greenhaven Press, P.O. Box 289009, San Diego, CA 92198-0009.

Campaign Financing: Politics and the Power of Money, by Suzanne M. Coil. (Issue & Debate Series). Grades 7 - 12. Published by Millbrook Press, 2 Old New Milford Rd., Brookfield, CT 06804. (800) 462-4703.

Image and Substance: The Media in U.S. Elections, by Victoria Sherrow. (Issue & Debate Series). Grades 7 - 12. Published by Millbrook Press, 2 Old New Milford Rd., Brookfield, CT 06804. (800) 462-4703.

The Right to Vote, by Bill Severn. Grades 8 - 12. Published by Ives Washburn, Inc., New York.

Elections: Locating the Author's Main Idea, by Neal Bernards. (Opposing Viewpoints Juniors Series). Grades 8 - 12 . Critical thinking and writing activities. Published by Greenhaven Press, Inc., PO Box 289009, San Diego, CA 92198-9009.

Reference Resources
Presidents

Scholastic Encyclopedia of the Presidents and Their Times, by David Rubel. Grades 4 - 12. Published by Scholastic, Inc., P.O. Box 7520, Jefferson City, MO 65102. (800) 325-6149.

The Buck Stops Here: The Presidents of the United States, by Alice Provensen. Grades 3 - 8. Published by HarperCollins Publications, 1000 Keystone Industrial Park, Scranton, PA 18512. (800) 328-3443.

The Founding Presidents: A Sourcebook on the U.S. Presidency, edited by Carter Smith. (American Albums From The Collections of The Library of Congress Series). Grades 5 - 10. Published by Millbrook Press, 2 Old New Milford Rd., Brookfield, CT 06804. (800) 462-4703. Other titles in the series include:

> *Presidents of a Young Republic*
> *Presidents of a Divided Nation*
> *Presidents of a Growing Country*
> *Presidents of a World Power*
> *Presidents in a Time of Change*

The Presidency, by Christine B. Scriabine. (Know Your Government Series). Grades 7 - 12. Published by Chelsea House Publishers, 1974 Sproul Rd., Suite 400, PO Box 914, Broomall, PA 19008. (800) 848-2665.

Our Presidency, by Karen Spies. (I Know America Series) Grades 3 - 8. Published by Millbrook Press, 2 Old New Milford Rd., Brookfield, CT 06804. (800) 462-4703.

Presidents in American History, by Charles A. Beard. Grades 6 - 10. Published by Silver Burdett Press, Simon & Schuster, Inc., 200 Old Tapan Rd., Old Tappan, NJ 07675.

I Can Be President, by Beatrice Beckman. Grades K - 3. Published by Children's Press, PO Box 1331, Danbury, CT 06813. (800) 621-1115.

Abraham Lincoln, by Ingri & Edgar D'Aulaire. Grades K - 4. (Picture Yearling Series). Published by Bantam, Doubleday, Dell, 2451 S. Wolf Rd., Des Plains, IL 60018. (800) 323-9872.

George Washington, by Ingri & Edgar D'Aulaire. Grades K - 4. (Picture Yearling Series). Published by Bantam, Doubleday, Dell, 2451 S. Wolf Rd., Des Plains, IL 60018. (800) 323-9872.

If You Grew Up With Abraham Lincoln, by Ann McGovern. Grades 2 - 6. Published by Scholastic Inc., 7502 Jefferson City, MO 65102. (800) 325-6149.

If You Grew Up With George Washington, by Ruth Gross. Grades 2 - 6. Published by Scholastic Inc., 7502 Jefferson City, MO 65102. (800) 325-6149.

Meet Thomas Jefferson, by Marvin Barrett. Grades 2 - 4. Published by Random House, 400 Hahn Rd., Westminster, MD 21157. (800) 733-3000.

Meet Abraham Lincoln, by Cary. Grades 2 - 4. Published by Random House, 400 Hahn Rd., Westminster, MD 21157. (800) 733-3000.

Meet George Washington, by Joan Heilbroner. Grades 2 - 4. Published by Random House, 400 Hahn Rd., Westminster, MD 21157. (800) 733-3000.

George Washington, by Brian Williams. (Children of History Series). Grades 1 - 5. Published by Marshall Cavendish Corporation, 99 Whiteplains Rd., P.O. Box 2001, Tarrytown, NY 10591-9001. (800) 821-9881.

Childhood of Famous Americans Series. Published by Simon & Schuster, owners of Macmillan Children's Book Group, 200 Old tappan Rd., Old Tappan, NJ 07675. (800) 257-5755. Titles suggested for this unit study include:

> ***George Washington: Young Leader***
> ***Martha Washington: America's First Lady***
> ***Abigail Adams: Girl of Colonial Days***
> ***Tom Jefferson: Third President of the U.S.***
> ***Abraham Lincoln: Great Emancipator***
> ***Mary Todd Lincoln: Girl of the Bluegrass***
> ***Teddy Roosevelt: Young Rough Rider***
> ***Eleanor Roosevelt: Fighter for Social Justice***

Harry S. Truman: Missouri Farm Boy
Dwight D. Eisenhower: Young Military Leader
John F. Kennedy: America's Youngest President

Sower Series, published by Mott Media, 1000 East Huron, Milford, MI 48381. (800) 421-6645. Grades 7 - 12. Titles suggested for this unit study include:

George Washington: Man of Courage and Prayer, by Norma C. Camp.
Abigail Adams: First Lady of Faith and Courage, by Evelyn Witter.
Abraham Lincoln, by David R. Collins.

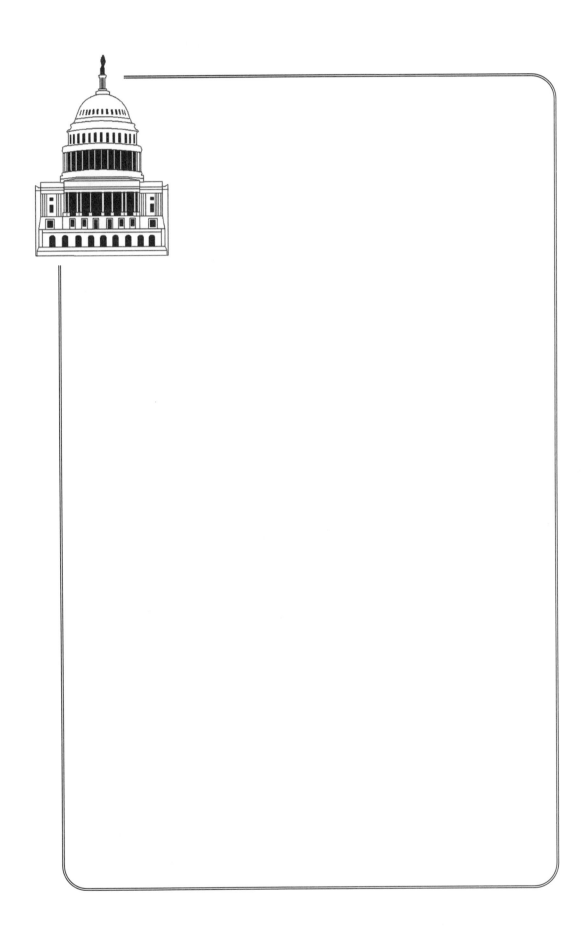

Reference Resources
Government

Land of Fair Play, Grades 7 - 8. Publishes by Christian Liberty Press, 502 West Euclid Avenue, Arlington heights, IL 60004. (708) 259-4444.

Civics For Today, by Margaret Branson. Grades 8 - 12. Published by Houghton Mifflin, Individual/Trade Division, 181 Ballardvale Rd., Wilmington, MA 01887.

How The White House Really Works, by George Sullivan. Grades 6 - 12. Published by Lodestar Books, E.P. Dutton, 2 Park Avenue, New York, NY 10016.

Whatever Happened to Justice?, by Richard Maybury. Published by Bluestocking Press, PO Box 2030, Shingle Spring, CA 95682-2030. (800) 959-8586.

The Constitution, by Richard B. Morris. (American History Topic Books). Grades 4 - 8. Published by Lerner Publications, 241 First Ave. N., Minneapolis, MN 55401. (800) 328-4929.

America's Great Document: The Constitution, by Donald E. Cooke. Grades 6 - 12. Published by Hammond Incorporated, 515 Valley St., Maplewood, NJ 07040. (800) 526-4953.

The Bill of Rights: How We Got It and What It Means, by Milton Meltzer. Grades 7 - 12. Published by Thomas Y. Crowell Junior Books, 10 E. 53rd Street, New York, NY 10022.

The Bill of Rights, by R. Conrad Stein. (Cornerstones of Freedom Series). Grades 2 - 5. Published by Children's Press, PO Box 1331, Danbury, CT 06813. (800) 621-1115.

If You Were There When They Signed The Constitution, by Elizabeth Levy. Grades 2 - 6. Published by Scholastic Inc., P.O. Box 7502, Jefferson City, MO 65102. (800) 325-6149.

The Federalist Papers by Alexander Hamilton, **James Madison and John Jay,** and **The Anti-Federalist Papers** by Patrick Henry and John DeWitt. Grades 7 - 12. Available from Elijah Company, Rt. 2; Box 100B, Crossville, TN 38555. (615) 456-6284.

Our Constitution, by Linda Carlson Johnson. (I Know America Series). Grades 3 - 8. Published by Millbrook Press, 2 Old New Milford Rd., Brookfield, CT 06804. (800) 462-4703.

The Making of the Constitution and **The Presidency,** Jackdaw Study Sets for grades 7 - 12. Available from Elijah Company, Rt. 2; Box 100B, Crossville, TN 38555. (615) 456-6284.

The President's Cabinet and How It Grew, by Nancy Winslow Parker. Grades 3 - 6. Published by Parents' Magazine Press, New York.

How You Can Influence Congress: The Complete Handbook For the Citizen Lobbyist, by George Alderson and Everett Sentman. Grades 10 and up. Published by E.P. Dutton, 2 Park Avenue, New York, NY 10016.

The Threat From Within: Unethical Politics and Politicians, by Michael Kronenwetter. Grades 10 - 12. Published by Franklin Watts, 5450 Cumberland Ave., Chicago, IL 60656. (800) 672-6672.

Presidents vs. Congress: Conflict and Compromise, by Edmund Lindop. Grades 9 - 12. Published by Franklin Watts, 5450 Cumberland Ave., Chicago, IL 60656. (800) 672-6672.

Press Versus Government: Constitutional Issues, by Donald J. Rogers. Grades 9 - 12. Published by Simon & Schuster, Inc., 200 Old Tappan Rd., Old Tappan, NJ 07675. (800) 223-2348.

Rights & Responsibilities: Using Your Freedom, by Francis Shuker-Haines. (Good Citizenship Series). Grades 4 - 7. Published by Raintree Steck-Vaughn, P.O. Box 26015, Austin, TX 78755. (800) 531-5015.

Government Nannies: The Cradle-To-Grave Agenda of Goals 2000 & Outcome-Based Education, by Cathy Duffy. Published by Noble Publishing. Available from Home Run Enterprises, 16172 Huxley Circle, Westminster, CA 92683.

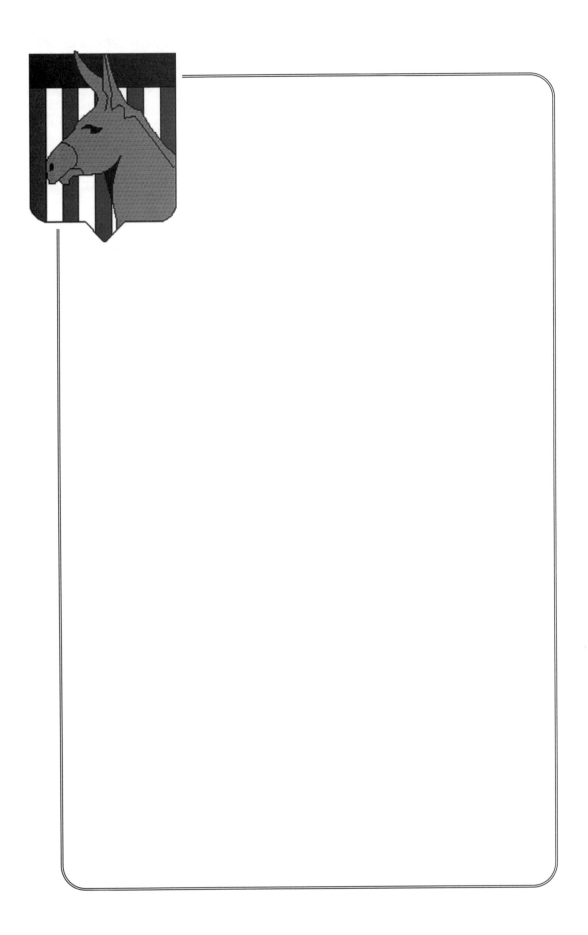

The First Book of the Constitution, by Richard B. Morris. Grade 2 - 6. Published by Franklin Watts, 5450 Cumberland Ave., Chicago, IL 60656. (800) 672-6672.

A More Perfect Union: The Story of Our Constitution, by Betsy and Giulio Maestro, Grade 2 - 6. Published by Mulberry Books, 105 Madison Avenue, New York, NY 10016.

Shh! We're Writing the Constitution, by Jean Fritz. Grade 2 - 6. The Putnam Publishing Group, 200 Madison Ave., New York, NY 10016. (800) 631-8571.

The President: America's Leaders, by Mary Oates Johnson. Grades 4 - 8. (Good Citizenship Series). Published by Raintree Steck-Vaughn, P.O. Box 26015, Austin, TX 78755. (800) 531-5015.

The Congress: American's Lawmakers, by Gary M. Stern. Grades 4 - 8. (Good Citizenship Series). Published by Raintree Steck-Vaughn, P.O. Box 26015, Austin, TX 78755. (800) 531-5015.

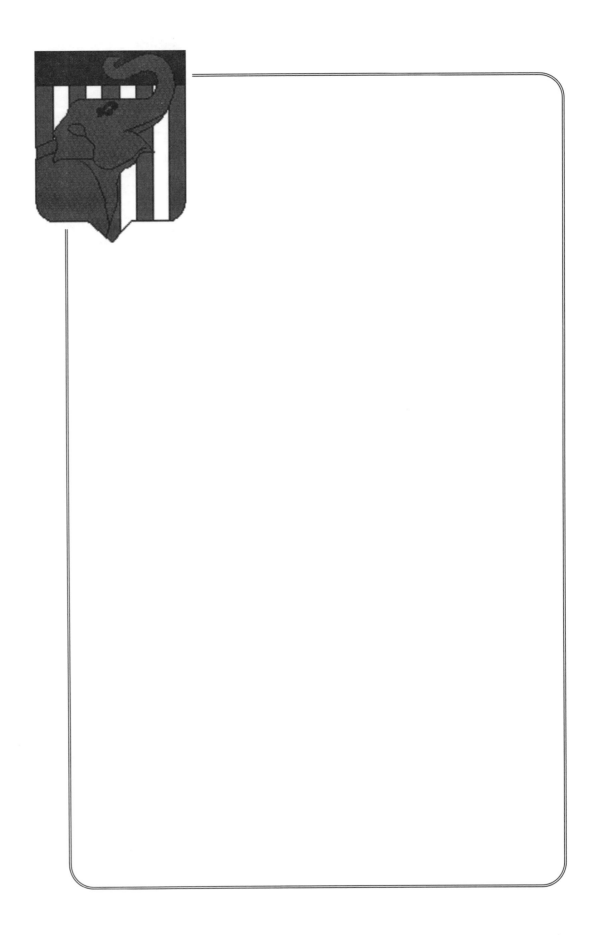

Reference Resources
Miscellaneous

The History of the White House, from Mallard Press. Grades 3 - 12. Published by BDD Promotional Book Co., 666 Fifth Ave., New York, NY 10103.

Profiles in Courage, by John F. Kennedy. Grades 7 and up. Published by Harper & Row, New York, NY. Available from the Elijah Company, Rt. 2, Box 100-B, Crossville, TN 38555. (615) 456-6284.

Are You Liberal? Conservative? Or Confused? by Richard Maybury. Published by Bluestocking Press, PO 2030, Shingle Springs, CA 93682-2030. (800) 959-8586.

Susan B. Anthony: Champion of Women's Rights, by Helen A. Monsell. (Childhood of Famous Americans Series). Published by Simon & Schuster, owners of Macmillan Children's Book Group, 200 Old Tappan Rd., Old Tappan, NJ 07675. (800) 257-5755.

Smithsonian Book of First Ladies, by Doris Faber. Grades 4 - 7. Published by Henry Holt & Company, 115 W. 18th Street, New York, NY 10011. (800) 488-5233.

Career Choices for the 90's: For Students of Political Science & Government, by Career Associates. Grades 9 and up. Published by Walker Publishing Company, 720 Fifth Ave., New York, NY 10019. (800) 289-2553.

Activity Resources

1. **Song of the U.S. Presidents,** an activity set that includes a cassette tape with songs, placemats and a game. Published by International Learning Systems. Available from Farm Country General Store, Rt. 1, Box 63, Metamora, IL 61548. (800) 551-FARM.

2. **Arguments,** critical thinking activities from Critical Thinking Press, P.O. Box 448, Pacific Grove, CA 93950. (800) 458-4849.

3. **The Story Behind the Scenery Series,** from KC Publications, P.O. Box 94558, Las Vegas, NV 89193-4558. (800) 626-9673. Available from Great Christian Books, (800) 775-5422. Titles in the series to consider for this unit study might include:

    Mount Rushmore
    Theodore Roosevelt National Park
    Lincoln Parks

4. For those of you interested in an in-depth study of American History using the unit study method, consider **A Study in American History for Ages 9 - 13,** by Jane Claire Lambert, author of the series **Five In a Row.** She has prepared a warm and exciting unit that will truly make American history come "alive" for your children. For more information, check with your favorite homeschool vendor, or write to:

    Jane Claire Lambert
    Five In a Row
    14901 Pinewood Drive
    Grandview, MO 64030-4509.

5. **Color the Patriotic Classics,** a patriotic book and tape set from Color the Classics. Available from Farm Country General Store, Rt. 1, Box 63, Metamora, IL 61548. (800) 551-FARM.

6. There are many activity books that might be of interest with this unit from Dover Publications, 31 East 2nd Street, Mineola, NY 11501. Some titles to consider are:

    American First Ladies Coloring Book
    Abraham Lincoln Family Paper Doll Set
    Harry S. Truman Family Paper Doll Set

7. ***Our Presidents*** and ***Flags - Washington to Lincoln,*** both from the Bellerophon coloring book series for grades 4 - 8. Published by Bellerophon Books, 122 Helena Ave., Santa Barbara, CA 93101.

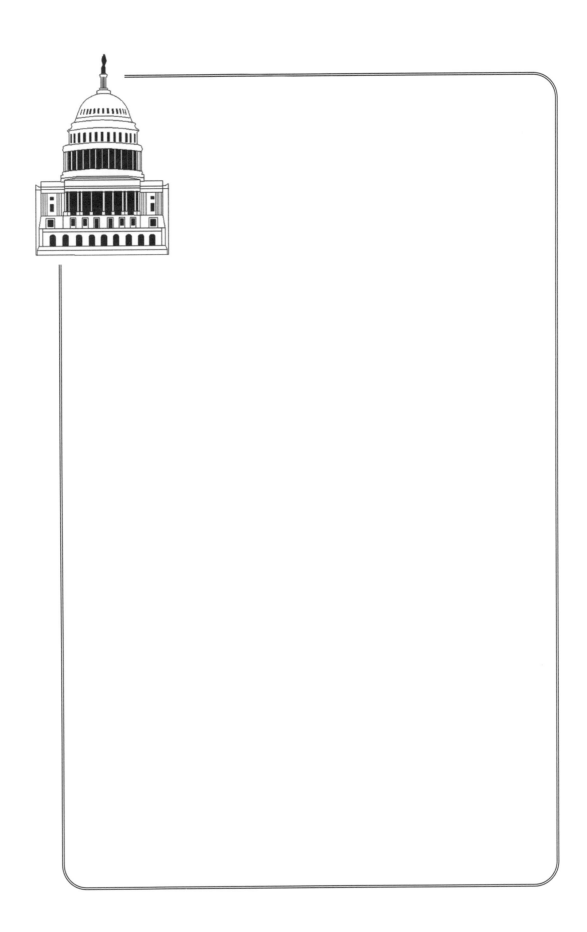

Reading Resources

George Washington's Breakfast, by Jean Fritz. Grades 2 - 4. Published by Coward-McCann, Inc., New York.

Just a Few Words, Mr. Lincoln: The Story of the Gettysburg Address, by Jean Fritz. Grades 2 - 4. Published by Grosset & Dunlap, part of the Putnam Publishing Group, 200 Madison Ave., New York, NY 10016. (800) 631-8571.

George Washington's Mother, by Jean Fritz. Grades 2 - 4. Published by Grosset & Dunlap, part of the Putnam Publishing Group, 200 Madison Ave., New York, NY 10016. (800) 631-8571.

The One Bad Thing About Father, by F. N. Monjo. (An I Can Read Book). Grades K - 4. Published by HarperCollins Publications, 1000 Keystone Industrial Park, Scranton, PA 18512. (800) 328-3443.

Yertle the Turtle & Other Stories, by Dr. Seuss. Grades PreK - 3. Published by Random House Books for Young Readers, 400 Hahn Rd., Westminster, MD 21157. (800) 733-3000.

Patriots' Days, by John Parlin. (A Holiday Book). Grades K - 6. Published by Garrard Publishing, Champaign, IL.

The Star-Spangled Banner, by Peter Spier. Grades K - 6. Published by Doubleday, a division of Bantam, Doubleday, Dell, 2451 S. Wolf Rd., Des Plains, IL 60018. (800) 223-6834. Available from Lifetime Books & Gifts, (800) 377-0390.

The White House Kids, by Rose Blue. Grades 5 - 8. Published by Millbrook Press, 2 Old New Milford Rd., Brookfield, CT 06804. (800) 462-4703.

Internet Resources

Here are some interesting sites on the Internet that you might want to visit while studying this unit. Please keep in mind that these pages, like all web pages, change from time to time. I recommend that you visit each site first, before the children do, to view the content and make sure that it meets your expectations. Also, use the **Subject Key Words** as search topics on Internet search engines, to find the latest additions that might pertain to this topic. (For help getting online, I highly recommend Homeschool Guide to the Online World — ISBN 1-888306-16-5.)

United States Congress
http://thomas.com

State Government Information Servers
http://www.law.indiana.edu/law/states.html

White House
http://www.whitehouse.gov

Project Vote Smart
gopher://chaos.dac.neu.edu:70/11/pvs-data

Library of Congress
http://lcweb.loc.gov

American Memory from the Library of Congress
http://rs6.loc.gov/amhome.html

American Historical Documents Archive—Univ. of Minnesota
gopher://joeboy.micro.umn.edu:70/11/Ebooks/By%20Title/Histdocs

Historical Documents and Speeches
gopher://dewey.lib.ncsu.edu:70/11/library/stacks/historical-documents-US

Yahoo - Reference:Libraries:Presidential Libraries
http://www.yahoo.com/Reference/Libraries/Presidential_Libraries/

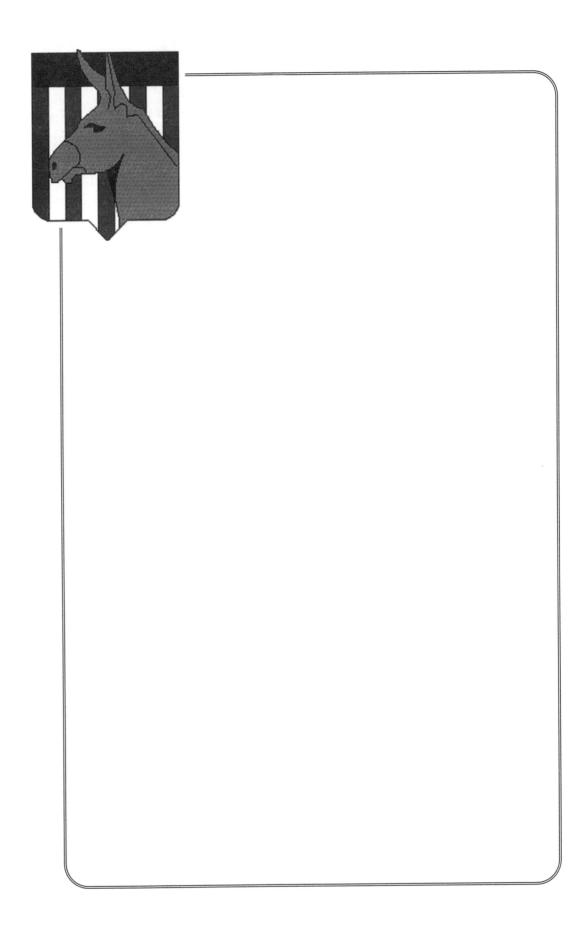

Election '96 Homepage
http://dodo.crown.net/%7Empg/election/96.html

1996 Parties and Presidential Candidates
http://dodo.crown.net/~mpg/election/parties.html

1996 Presidential Election
http://www.libertynet.org/%7Eucrc/pres96.html

Democratic National Committee
http://www.democrats.org/

The 1996 Presidential Election
http://republicans.vt.com/pe1996.html

Information Headquarters for the Republican Primary
http://www.umr.edu/~sears/primary/main.html

1996 Republican National Convention Center—San Diego
http://www.sddt.com/files/convention.html

Yahoo - Government:Politics:Elections:1996 U.S. Elections
http://www.yahoo.com/Government/Politics/Elections/1996_U_S__Elections/

Yahoo - Government:Politics:Elections
http://www.yahoo.com/Government/Politics/Elections/

Campaign Central Homepage
http://www.clark.net/ccentral/

Almanac of American Politics
http://politicsusa.com/PoliticsUSA/resources/almanac/

PoliticsUSA Issues Comparison
http://politicsusa.com/PoliticsUSA/issues/

PoliticsUSA Resources
http://politicsusa.com/PoliticsUSA/resources/

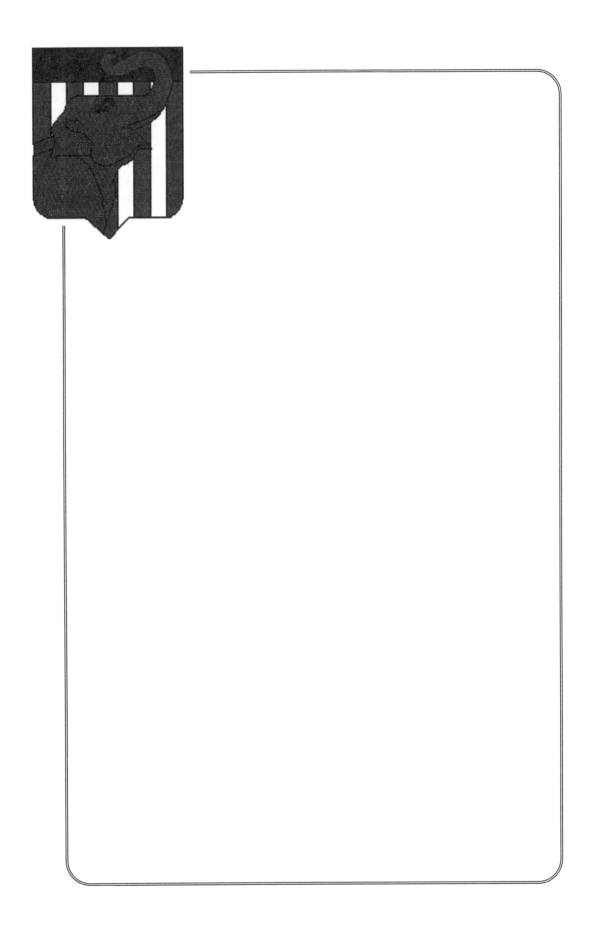

ElectNet: Welcome
http://www.e1.com/GOV/gov.html
League Of Women Voters of Iowa Home Page
http://lwvia.cornell-iowa.edu/

Executive Branch Information Services
http://lwvia.cornell-iowa.edu/FedGov/ExecutiveBranch.html

Legislative Branch Information Services
http://lwvia.cornell-iowa.edu/FedGov/LegislativeBranch.html

Congressional State Term Limits
http://www.termlimits.org/

PAC contributions for 1994 candidates
gopher://c-span.org/11/Resource/fec

Presidential Sites Idea Network
http://sunsite.unc.edu/lia/president/pressites/pressites.html

Presidents
http://sunsite.unc.edu/lia/president/pressites/PresidentS-res.html

Inaugural Addresses of the Presidents
http://www.cc.columbia.edu/acis/bartleby/inaugural/index.html

U.S. Chess Federation
http://dab.psi.net/uscbrowser/uscf-info.html

Amanda Bennett's Unit Study Web Page:
http://www.gocin.com/unit_study/

Working Outline

I. Introduction

    A. The meaning and origin of the word "election"

    B. Why it is important to study and understand elections

        1. To understand how the government framework is designed to work

        2. To learn about the history of our country and its elected officials

        3. To understand the campaign process, candidates' viewpoints and the importance of issues

        4. To become a part of the American government, by voicing opinions and convictions to our representatives at all levels

II. Government basics

    A. The Constitution

        1. The drafting of the Constitution

            a. The convention and attending delegates

b. Plans proposed for the new agreement

2. The Great Compromise

3. Ratification

4. The Bill of Rights

5. Constitutional Amendments

B. Three main branches of American government

   1. Executive Branch

      a. President

      b. Vice President

      c. Cabinet

   2. Legislative Branch

      a. House of Representatives

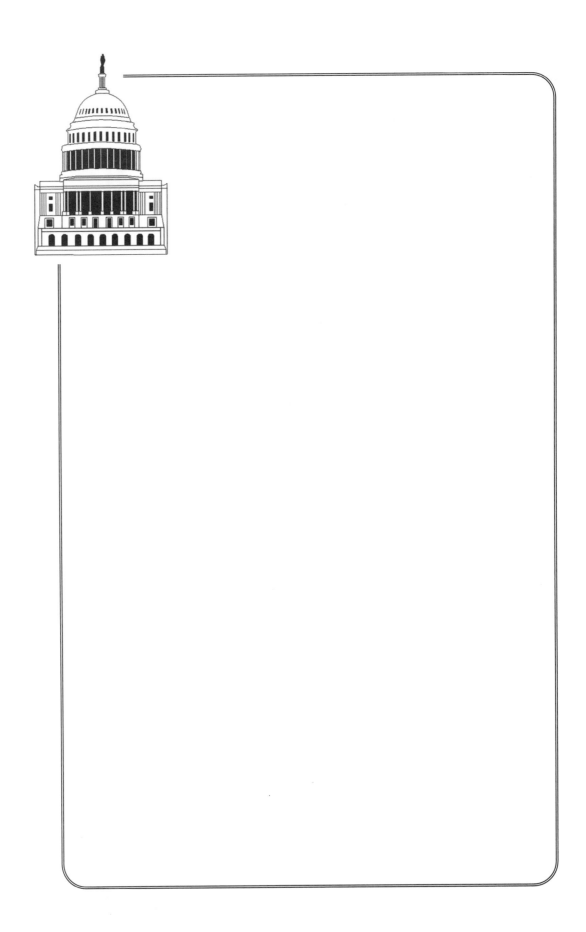

        b.   Senate

   3.   Judicial Branch

        a.   Supreme Court

        b.   Federal Court System

III.   Government by representation

A.   The right to vote

   1.   Voting was originally restricted to white men that owned property or had considerable wealth

   2.   The Fifteenth Amendment to the Constitution

        a.   This amendment made it illegal to block citizens from voting because of race

        b.   Poll tax and literacy tests were used to get around this amendment

   3.   The Nineteenth Amendment to the Constitution gave women the right to vote

4. The Twenty-fourth Amendment to the Constitution forbid the use of poll tax to deny a citizen the right to vote

5. The Twenty-sixth Amendment lowered the minimum voting age to eighteen years of age.

B. National elections

1. Presidential elections

a. Popular vote election

b. Electoral College vote

2. Congressional elections

3. Election Day—the first Tuesday after the first Monday in November

C. State elections

1. Governor

2. State congressional representatives

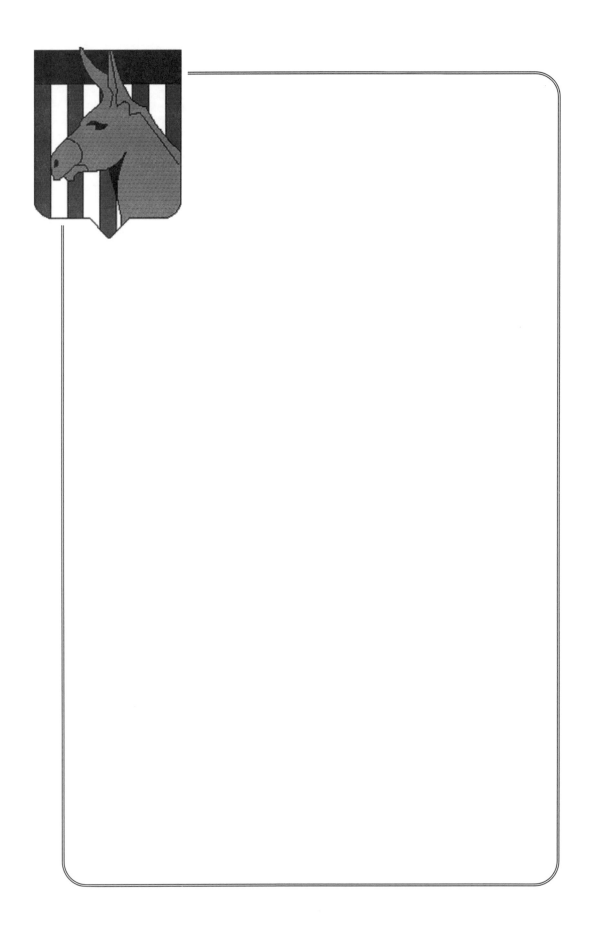

3.   State offices

    a.   Insurance Commissioner

    b.   Treasury

D.   Local elections

  1.   Commissioners

  2.   Mayor

  3.   Sheriff

  4.   Local issues

    a.   Zoning/Planning

    b.   Taxes

    c.   Referendums

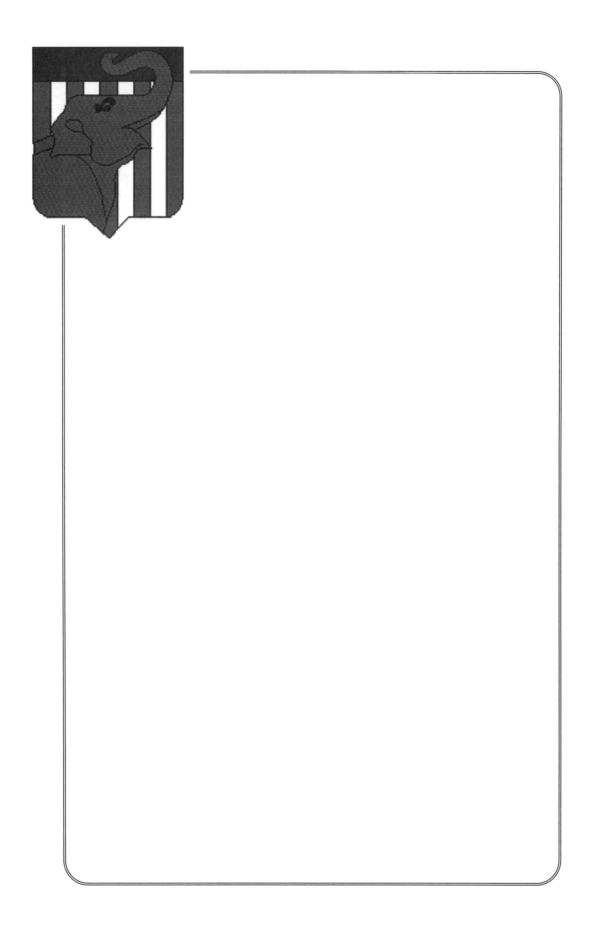

E.   Special elections

IV.   The structure of an election

A.   Political parties

    1.   Platform

    2.   Candidates

    3.   Voter appeal

    4.   Caucuses and primaries

B.   Candidates

    1.   Must meet qualifications for the desired position

        a.   President

        b.   Senate seat

        c.   House of Representatives seat

2. Develop their stances on various key election issues

    a. Laws

    b. Taxes

    c. Rights

    d. Economy

    e. Goals

    f. Special interests

C. Campaigns

    1. Notable historic campaigns

        a. Election of Thomas Jefferson in 1800—two-party system is firmly established

        b. Election of Andrew Jackson in 1828—marking the beginning of the importance of the popular vote

    c.   Election of Abraham Lincoln in 1860—split the party system and marked the beginning of the secession of Southern states

2.   Structure of a campaign

    a.   Local or state election

    b.   National election

3.   The campaign process for the candidate

    a.   Organize a campaign staff

        (1)   Campaign manager

        (2)   Advance team

        (3)   Media contact

        (4)   Fund-raiser

        (5)   Speech writer

    b.   Begin fund-raising efforts

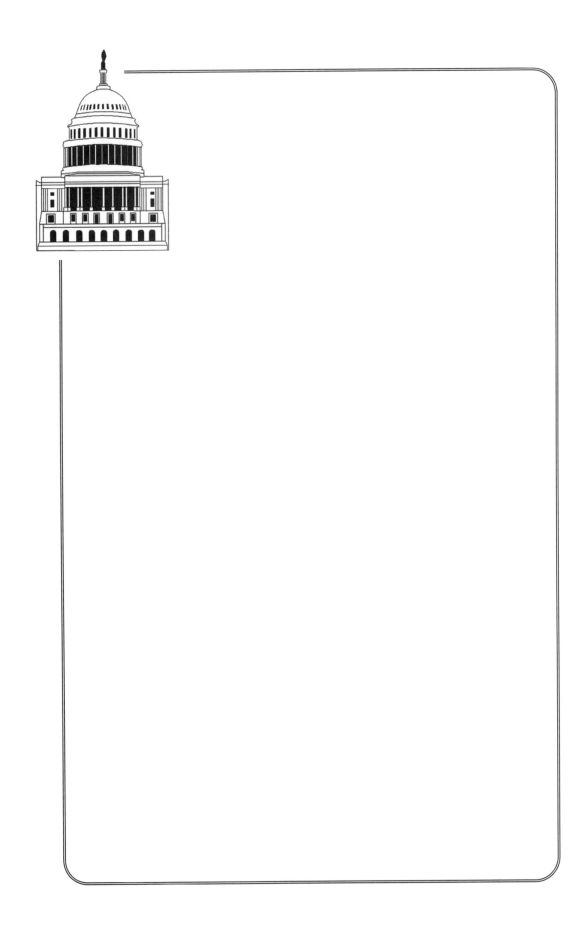

     c.   Develop an agenda and issues position

     d.   Consult with a pollster to get feedback on issues relevant to your constituents

     e.   Meet with the public

          (1)   Develop recognition

          (2)   Get feedback on issues

          (3)   Test new ideas

          (4)   Refine political image

4.   Raising financing for the campaign

     a.   Federal Elections Campaign Act (1971)

     b.   Political action committees (PACs)

     c.   Candidate's personal efforts and funds

     d.   Political party efforts

       e.   Reporting to the Federal Elections Commission

V. Voting

A.   Definition of "vote" and "suffrage"

B.   Each citizen's opportunity to have an impact on our government

    1.   Right to vote is guaranteed

    2.   History of the vote

        a.   Early American voting procedures

        b.   Australian ballot acceptance

C.   Voter registration

    1.   Eligible voters

        a.   Residency requirements

        b.   18 years of age or older

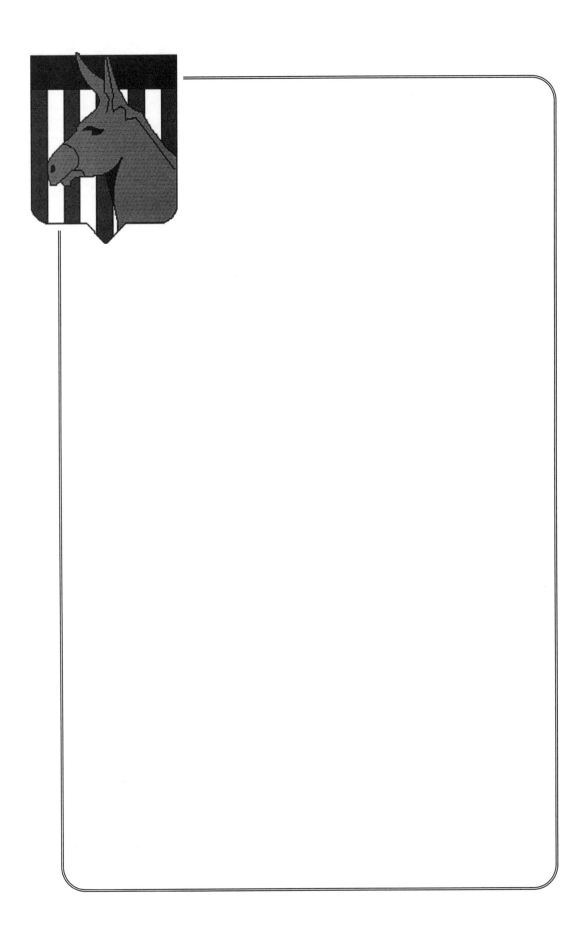

2. Ineligible voters

    a. Citizens of other countries

    b. People convicted of felonies

    c. Mentally incompetent people

D. Casting the vote

    1. The voting machines

    2. The ballot

    3. Absentee ballot

E. The vote count

F. Reporting the election results

    1. Media coverage

    2. Victory and defeat speeches

VI. American Political Parties

A. History of political parties in America

   1. Federalist party

   2. Anti-Federalist party

   3. Democratic Republican party

   4. National Republican party

   5. Democratic party

   6. Whig party

B. Modern-day political parties

   1. Republican party

   2. Democratic party

   3. Third parties

VII. Presidents of the United States

A. George Washington

    1. In office from 1789 - 1797

    2. Elected unanimously by the Electoral College

B. John Adams

    1. In office from 1797 - 1801

    2. Federalist Party

C. Thomas Jefferson

    1. In office from 1801 - 1809

    2. Democratic-Republican Party

D. James Madison

    1. In office from 1809 - 1817

    2. Democratic-Republican Party

E.   James Monroe

   1.   In office from 1817 - 1825

   2.   Democratic-Republican Party

F.   John Quincy Adams

   1.   In office from 1825 - 1829

   2.   Democratic-Republican Party

G.   Andrew Jackson

   1.   In office from 1829 - 1837

   2.   Democratic Party

H.   Martin Van Buren

   1.   In office from 1837 - 1841

   2.   Democratic Party

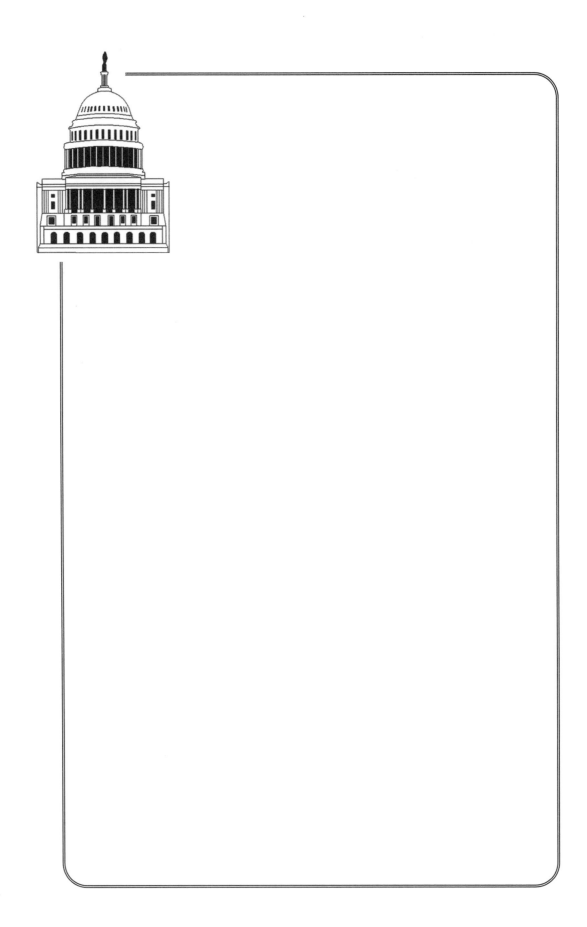

I. William Henry Harrison

    1. In office 1841

    2. Whig Party

J. John Tyler

    1. In office from 1841 - 1845

    2. Whig Party

K. James K. Polk

    1. In office from 1845 - 1849

    2. Democratic Party

L. Zachary Taylor

    1. In office from 1849 - 1850

    2. Whig Party

M.   Millard Fillmore

   1.   In office from 1850 - 1853

   2.   Whig Party

N.   Franklin Pierce

   1.   In office from 1853 - 1857

   2.   Democratic Party

O.   James Buchanan

   1.   In office from 1857 - 1861

   2.   Democratic Party

P.   Abraham Lincoln

   1.   In office from 1861 - 1865

   2.   Republican Party

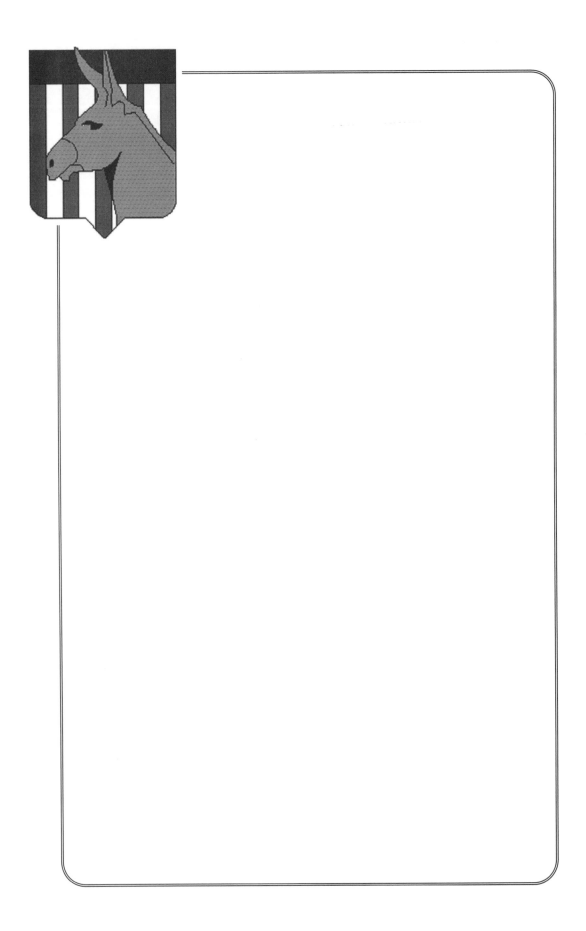

Q. Andrew Johnson

    1. In office from 1865 - 1869

    2. Democratic Party

R. Ulysses S. Grant

    1. In office from 1869 - 1877

    2. Republican Party

S. Rutherford B. Hayes

    1. In office from 1877 - 1881

    2. Republican Party

T. James A. Garfield

    1. In office in 1881

    2. Republican Party

U.   Chester A. Arthur

    1.   In office from 1881 - 1885

    2.   Republican Party

V.   Grover Cleveland

    1.   In office from 1885 - 1889, and again from 1893 - 1897

    2.   Democratic Party

W.   Benjamin Harrison

    1.   In office from 1889 - 1893

    2.   Republican Party

X.   William McKinley

    1.   In office from 1897 - 1901

    2.   Republican Party

Y.   Theodore Roosevelt

  1.   In office from 1901 - 1909

  2.   Republican Party

Z.   William H. Taft

  1.   In office from 1909 - 1913

  2.   Republican Party

AA.   Woodrow Wilson

  1.   In office from 1913 - 1921

  2.   Democratic Party

BB.   Warren G. Harding

  1.   In office from 1921 - 1923

  2.   Republican Party

CC. Calvin Coolidge

    1.   In office from 1923 - 1929

    2.   Republican Party

DD. Herbert Hoover

    1.   In office from 1929 - 1933

    2.   Republican Party

EE. Franklin D. Roosevelt

    1.   In office from 1933 - 1945

    2.   Democratic Party

FF. Harry S. Truman

    1.   In office from 1945 - 1953

    2.   Democratic Party

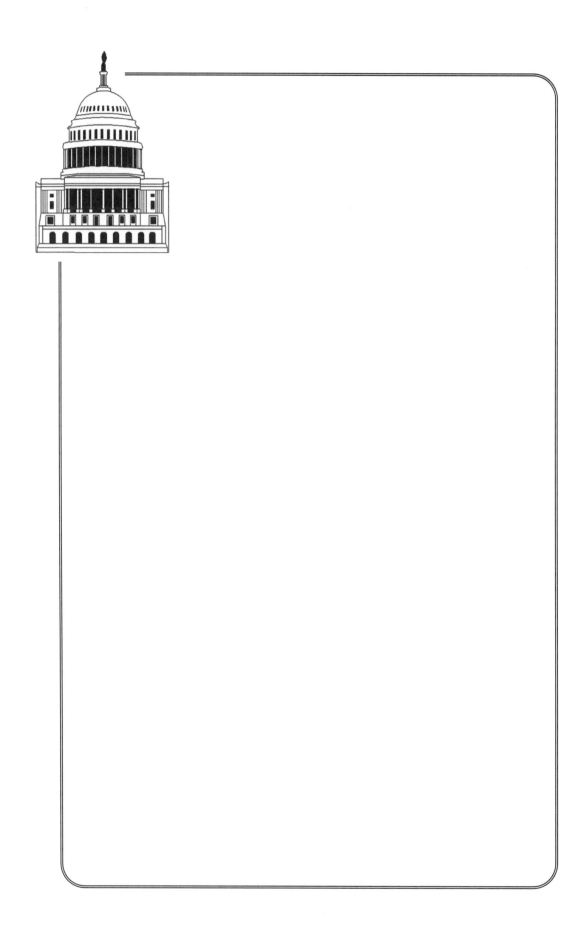

GG. Dwight D. Eisenhower

    1.   In office from 1953 - 1961

    2.   Republican Party

HH. John F. Kennedy

    1.   In office from 1961 - 1963

    2.   Democratic Party

II. Lyndon B. Johnson

    1.   In office from 1963 - 1969

    2.   Democratic Party

JJ. Richard M. Nixon

    1.   In office from 1969 - 1974

    2.   Republican Party

KK. Gerald R. Ford

    1.   In office from 1974 - 1977

    2.   Republican Party

LL. Jimmy Carter

    1.   In office from 1977 - 1981

    2.   Democratic party

MM. Ronald Reagan

    1.   In office from 1981 - 1989

    2.   Republican Party

NN. George Bush

    1.   In office from 1989 - 1993

    2.   Republican Party

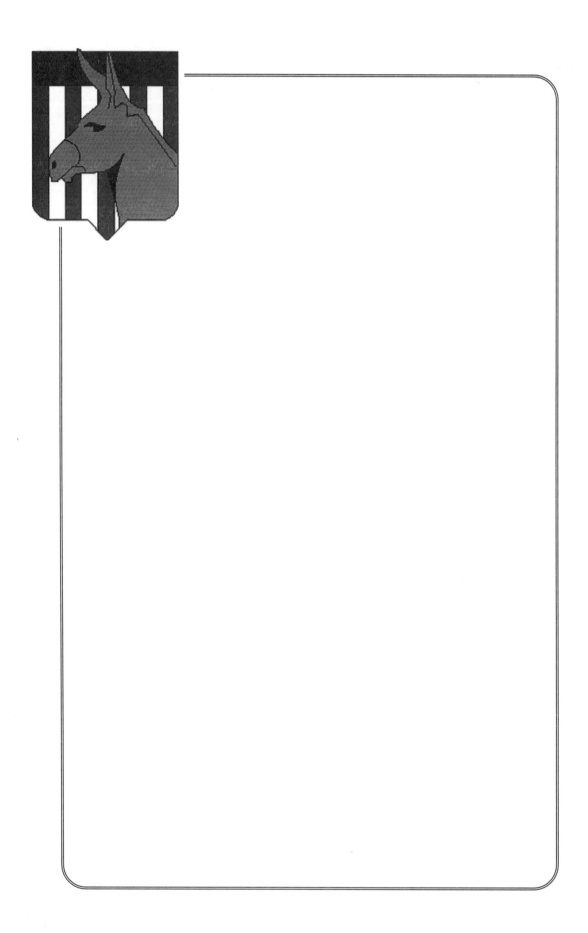

OO. William Clinton

    1. In office from 1993 - present

    2. Democratic Party

VIII. The arts and elections

A. Campaign designs—buttons, banners, etc.

B. Musical slogans, songs, etc.

C. Candidate images—photos, paintings, media portrayal

D. Collectible campaign items

About The Author

Amanda Bennett, author and speaker, wife and mother of three, holds a degree in mechanical engineering. She has written this ever-growing series of unit studies for her own children, to capture their enthusiasm and nurture their gifts and talents. The concept of a thematic approach to learning is a simple one. Amanda will share this simplification through her books, allowing others to use these unit study guides to discover the amazing world that God has created for us all.

Science can be a very intimidating subject to teach, and Amanda has written this series to include science with other important areas of curriculum that apply naturally to each topic. The guides allow more time to be spent enjoying the unit study, instead of spending weeks of research time to prepare for each unit. She has shared the results of her research in the guides, including plenty of resources for areas of the study, spelling and vocabulary lists, fiction and nonfiction titles, possible careers within the topic, writing ideas, activity suggestions, addresses of manufacturers, teams, and other helpful resources.

The science-based series of guides currently includes the Unit Study Adventures titles:

Baseball	Homes
Computers	Oceans
Elections	Olympics
Electricity	Pioneers
Flight	Space
Gardens	Trains

The holiday-based series of guides currently includes the Unit Study Adventures titles:

Christmas
Thanksgiving

This planned 40-book series will soon include additional titles, which will be released periodically. We appreciate your interest. "Enjoy the Adventure."